GYMNASTICS

Planning an Exhibition

RIK FEENEY
Richardson Publishing

Gymnastics: Planning an Exhibition
by Rik Feeney
usabookcoach@gmail.com
www.RickFeeney.com
www.PublishingSuccessOnline.com

RICHARDSON PUBLISHING
PO Box 162115
Altamonte Springs, FL 32716

DISCLAIMER

This document is written and intended to be used by USAG professional level gymnastics coaches who also have current USAG Safety Certification. The publisher and author are not engaged in the profession of rendering any form of legal, medical, or accounting advice. If for any reason legal, medical, or accounting advice is necessary, you should seek out qualified professionals.

The purpose of this document is to educate and acquaint individuals with basic techniques for preparing gymnastics exhibitions and demonstrate how to use creative ideas to improve business.

Every effort has been made to provide complete and accurate information on this subject. Please send requests for additional information to Richardson Publishing. If possible, such requests will be answered in future editions of this document.

The author and Richardson Publishing shall have neither liability nor responsibility to any person or entity with respect to any loss or damage caused or alleged to be caused directly or indirectly by the information contained in this document.

Inside illustrations:
Presentation Task Force CGM V4.0

The safety of the athlete, coaches, parents, and spectators is always the paramount concern in any gymnastics activity whether it is in a gymnastics facility or at an exhibition venue.

INTRODUCTION

The following document deals with a topic that is familiar to anyone who has been involved with the sport of gymnastics or cheerleading.

In fact, as you read this document you may say to yourself *"I remember when something like that happened to me."* (while at an exhibition).

My hallucination is that you and I are probably very much alike. I bet you have enough of the entrepreneurial spirit that you are either a head coach or a club owner / director.

The sport of gymnastics and/or cheerleading infected and affected you; now it is in your blood to stay.

I am also willing to bet you are at least in part a "perfectionist." You want the job to get done right the first time. Because of that feeling, you probably take on more responsibility than other members of your staff.

I am the same way.

Over the years, I took on most of the tasks associated with running a gymnastics facility. I was doing most of the work. I was coach, instructor, substitute instructor, payroll clerk, marketing director, camp counselor, yada, yada, yada… I had no time left for myself to enjoy the fruits of my labor.

One day in a flash of inspiration (or was it desperation?) I decided to get my staff involved with all levels of the business. I understood that if I was still going to be a quasi-perfectionist, I would have to develop patience and let others make the mistakes necessary to learn the jobs I would now delegate.

The only problem; this sport has a high turnover in employees as they go off to college, move to other gyms, or set up their own facilities. My business could not afford to start at ground zero each time a new employee was brought on-board. (This is only slightly exaggerated.)

To solve this problem, I decided to put together a series of documents like the one you have right now.

Each document details how to accomplish some aspect of the business and sport of gymnastics. Now, I could delegate a series of jobs and know that my staff had all the information they needed at their fingertips, right?

Well, it didn't work out quite as smoothly as that. I still have to answer questions and check up on new staff members, but a major portion of my time spent teaching the process has been eliminated. I now have a few more hours a week to indulge in other activities like going to the beach or taking a nap.

I hope this document helps to achieve the same goal - more time for you.

In addition, it should help you save money. Consider what your time is worth on an hourly basis. Wouldn't it be less expensive to have one of your employees do this job for you?

After all, the whole purpose of having employees is to duplicate yourself and what you have to offer to the public.

I would like to thank you personally for purchasing this document.

I hope it helps you achieve more in your business and gives you more time to do more of what you want.

Please write to me care of the publisher's address if you have any ideas you feel should be added to this document or could be a subject of other gymnastics documents.

Planning an Exhibition

All your team members have shown up at the mall on time looking really sharp in their new leotards.

Your team parents are helping to keep the crowd of spectators out of the display area.

Everyone is finished warming up, the show is about to begin.

You finish connecting the wires on your CD player or portable IPOD system, then go to plug it in...

Where is the electrical outlet?

After a frantic search, you find there isn't one in the immediate vicinity. The team is looking at you expectantly ready to begin their routine.

The crowd is getting restless and their attention is returning to all the errands they have to finish.

In due course, the crowd begins to thin out and by the time you have secured an extension cord, most of your audience is gone.

You end up doing the exhibition for your team parents.

Proper Planning

Most coaches can relate to the above situation or situations similar.

The forgotten CD, a stage that is too short for the routine, or worse elevated off the ground, and entrances to the exhibition area that are too small to fit your equipment through.

The possible problems are endless, but you can prevent most by adequate planning before the event.

I am not going to show you how to run major shows at Madison Square Garden. Such shows would require ticket sales, concessions, security, and a litany of other concerns and details that boggle the mind.

Instead, this document lists several important topics to consider when running the average exhibition in your local community.

Now Performing In the Center Ring!

Most clubs do not have the luxury of specialized exhibition teams.

Competitive team members usually cover the bill.

Using recreational class members is another good idea. Using both groups shows the public both ends of the gymnastics spectrum.

The key is to pick those youngsters who like showing off in front of a crowd.

Note: If you have gymnasts that get a bad case of nerves before a competition, doing exhibitions might be the answer to developing their confidence in a low pressure, fun filled way.

Most exhibition routines are prepared in relation to the team or class level performing.

For special occasions, you may want to specifically choreograph tumbling and dance routines.

For the average display, my teams usually have a standard routine we whip into shape within a few days' notice of the exhibition.

To keep the routines fresh in memory, I incorporate the exhibition routines into practice every few weeks and decide on any changes based on the number of gymnasts able to attend.

Don't get too fancy with your exhibitions because circumstances can change.

If you place one team member, or team level in a key role and they can't make it that could blow your whole presentation.

A similar result can happen focusing on one piece of apparatus to carry the show.

Flexibility is the key word when running exhibitions.

Changing numbers of gymnasts, site constraints, and the type of equipment used help determine the final product.

You know the old saying about the best laid plans of mice and men...

I Meant To Do That!

Most audience members are not well educated in the sport of gymnastics or cheerleading so there are a lot of things that can be put over on them.

I remember some exhibitions where everything possible that could go wrong did go wrong and the audience still loved it.

I received a lot of positive comments afterwards.

Mess ups handled smoothly can add enjoyment to the exhibition. I plan routines now with purposefully choreographed wipeouts (safely done!) just for the audience reaction.

You may also want to add a little comedy to your routine to spice it up.

Every team has at least one entertainer. Work up some special situation you can use to get laughs during the exhibition.

Whatever you do in the exhibition, the key is to leave the audience wanting more.

If you fully satisfy the crowds desire, they may walk away content and not seek anymore information about your club.

Leave the audience desiring more and invite them to your club to get it.

Of course, you better remember to bring club brochures and "free" lesson coupons to hand out by team members after the show.

Note: Let the team members hand out the marketing info. They will appreciate the comments from the spectators, and the spectators will enjoy meeting these amazing athletes!

Special Instructions

From time to time there may be a trick missed that causes a break in tumbling or your dance routine.

You may want to develop a special set of instructions in case that happens.

For example, someone falls on a front tuck off mini-tramp, the next person knows to veer off and not go for the trick.

Developing a set of hand signals is also a good idea. Each athlete can look to the coach for a clue. A clenched fist means to tuck, twirling the index finger means to do a full twist, and so on.

Back to Square One

One of the main concerns in doing an exhibition is what equipment to bring.

Obviously, this is determined by site constraints or the specific request of the group for whom you are doing the exhibition.

In general, take the least amount of equipment possible while maintaining appropriate safety standards. While you may have several willing hands to get you to the site and set up, parents and gymnasts seem to disappear at the end when everything needs to be packed up.

It is a good idea to schedule specifically who will set up and break down the equipment.

Vehicles for transporting the equipment may also have an effect on how much and what type of equipment you can bring with you.

Be sure the vehicles can safely "contain" the equipment.

Stacking equipment on top of vehicles is not a good idea. Mats and other apparatus blown off while driving to the site can cause quite a commotion on the highway and rearrange your equipment into new and different shapes that could be difficult to work with later.

Be sure to bring chalk, tools for setting equipment and repairing the apparatus.

When doing outdoor exhibitions always carry a tarp or some type of plastic covering.

The weather could change at a moments notice and ruin suede beams or vault tables and make a mess of everything.

Post it on your website

Communicate important information on directions, times, and what to wear directly to the parents and team members.

Put it in writing, and especially post on the gym club's web site so anyone with a cell phone can access the information 24 hours a day, 7 days a week in case someone forgets.

You may also want to put a contact number, probably the gym's, so anyone running late or someone who is lost can let you know.

Site Plan

Previous to any exhibition you should go and visit the site where your athletes will be performing. Determine the:

- size of the area;

- possible obstructions;

- location of the nearest electrical outlet.

- You may want to sketch out a diagram of the area (to scale) to make sure the demonstration you have planned will work in the designated area.

CRITICAL!: Check where the *little girls room* is for changing clothes and for those gymnasts who get excited before the show and need to use it in a hurry.

While checking the exhibition site be sure to note the **nearest parking** area and **entrance** for your team members and parents. Be sure they know exactly where to go when they arrive.

Some additional items to check on include:

• Check to see whether a permit is necessary, and where and from whom you can get it.

• At county fairs, malls, and other such demonstrations, you may need to bring equipment in before the public arrives. Check on the times when you can set up or bring in your equipment.

You may also have to leave your equipment in place until the public leaves for safety reasons. Find out when you can break down your equipment to take it back to your gym.

• Check for storage areas and methods of securing your equipment when not in use.

• Call your insurance agent to check your club's liability insurance policy.

Many locations ask for a **certificate of insurance** before allowing you to put on a display. Your agent can send you the necessary certificates.

Make sure the policy covers you, your gymnasts, your equipment, spectators, and possibly the premises while out at a display.

Timing Is Everything

Once you have checked the site, you need to figure out the timing of your show.

The best exhibitions run quickly from one event to the next.

Use lively commentary to hold audience interest while preparing the next segment of your show.

Set a schedule for equipment set up, gymnast warm up, introduction, the exhibition itself (I.E. dance numbers, equipment demonstrations, special numbers, club information), and finally the closing.

An exhibition should run thirty to forty-five minutes. It may need some trimming to clean it up, or rearrange the sequence of events so equipment changes are smooth and efficient.

Always do a full dress rehearsal before the actual event to iron out potential problems.

May I Present For Your Entertainment...

To keep the exhibition running smoothly, have an announcer give running commentary on the action like they do on Monday Night Football.

If you don't like talking on the microphone, or you need to spot a trick, enlist a parent or another coach for the job.

Before the exhibition, sit down and write what you want your announcer to say on index cards or a sheet of paper.

Provide "color" or background information on each of your gymnasts like: where they live (town only, not actual residence), level of competition, favorite apparatus, hobbies and goals, special awards received, and maybe a favorite quote. As they perform in the exhibition you can relate this information to the audience.

When planning your commentary, remember your audience does not understand most gymnastics terminology.

Use simple terms, even if they are technically incorrect.

It is also helpful to explain by demonstration the different body positions (I.E. squat, pike, straddle, layout) so your audience will know what to expect.

Describe particular items of interest on each of the events.

Many people watch gymnastics on TV and have no idea how to score a gymnastic routine, especially with the new scoring system!

A brief discussion on what composes a score, the difference between compulsory and optional routines, age levels, and competition levels will help keep audience interest.

Items like this are ideal to use when shifting equipment and the crowd is waiting for the next portion of your demonstration.

If I Set It Up, Will They Come?

At malls and other locations check the "in house" advertising policies.

It may be possible to have your demonstration advertised on the marquee outside the mall or store.

In addition, ask someone in the mall public relations office to announce your exhibition in newspaper ads with their regularly scheduled advertising as a perk to entice the public.

In any case, you should always send a news release with a picture of your team to the local newspaper, radio, and TV station.

Keep press kits handy for any media that happen to turn up on the day of your show.

On the day of your exhibition, advertise the times your team will perform.

Place little placards listing the time of the next exhibition around your display area and have exhibition times announced via the P.A. system if possible.

Part of the importance of an exhibition is to entice people to come to see your club and hopefully enroll their children.

Be sure to have plenty of club brochures and application forms to hand out after every exhibit.

You may want to give out promotional items like pens, stickers, or maybe even T-shirts that have your club name, address, email, website, and especially your phone number on them.

Just In Case

Always bring medical releases and emergency information on each of your gymnasts that include home and emergency phone numbers.

Prepare an action plan with your coaches and parents in case an accident occurs during the exhibition.

How you handle such a situation will quickly relay your level of professionalism and safety concern to the public.

Note: Always bring some type of cooling agent like ice or one of the chemical ice packs in case of bumps and bruises.

Some other ideas to promote safety:

• Place ropes or flags around the exhibition area so spectators cannot interfere with the display.

• Keep the mats covered during outdoor exhibitions when not in use, or the sun will bake some behinds when the show starts.

• If it is fairly hot, be sure the team members have plenty to drink. Have them stay cool in the shade so they won't suffer from heat exhaustion or dehydration.

• Plan breaks between shows so the gymnasts can have something to eat well in advance of the next show so there are no surprise demonstrations.

• During the show, all gym bags and equipment not being used should be out of sight so as not to clutter the visual display nor cause accidental injury when tripped over.

Special Note:

If you plan to use some portion of exhibition time for a "free spectator experience" (like a Sunday-in-the-Park), bring participation waivers with you and get them signed by legal guardians and/or participants before allowing anyone on the equipment.

Check with your insurance agent for specific wording to cover you and your program in case of possible injury to a participant.

On with the Show

Not all displays require such extensive planning, but it is good to go through this list each time to be sure.

There are situations unique and sometimes unexpected to deal with at each exhibition.

Depending on its location and purpose, there may be other factors you need to consider.

Advance preparation in every case will help you and your gymnasts perform under the best possible conditions for the safety and enjoyment of all concerned.

Now that you have a plan, get out there and knock their socks off!

EXHIBITION CHECKLIST

I. Exhibition Agenda

- Newsletter to parents re: times and dates

- Map with directions to exhibition site

- Confirmation of gymnasts attending exhibition

- Staff scheduled to help with exhibition (& watch the gym)

- Press release / public notice sent out about exhibition.

- Radio / TV stations notified previous and on the day of the show

II. **Gymnastics Equipment.**

- Transport vehicle arranged to and from exhibition site.

- Equipment list prepared and approved by gym director.

- Set up and breakdown crew assembled.

- Tools for repairs and set up loaded.

- Tarps to cover equipment from rain and / or direct sunshine.

- Clean up materials for equipment (rags, mops, etc.)

- Gym chalk

III. **Exhibition Site**

• Site map prepared with exhibition layout.

• Permits (if required) obtained and packed with supplies.

• Clean up crew assembled. (before and after show)

• Parking facilities reserved for equipment transport / gymnasts?

• Storage area identified (for equipment before, after, and between shows)

IV. **Sound Equipment**

• Microphone, bullhorn, or public address system

• Stereo or cassette deck and speakers

• Electrical outlets previously identified? (Extension cords?)

• Equipment operators identified for CD player (lights?)

• Announcer or commentator

• Script for the exhibition

• CD's of exhibition music

V. **Insurance & Medical Emergency**

- Certificate of insurance (if necessary)

- Medical release forms for all gymnasts attending exhibition

- Emergency phone numbers for all gymnasts

- First aid kit checked for supplies and packed with equipment

Double check:

- Chemical ice packs, gym tape, ace bandages, splints, Band-Aids

- Emergency plan established in case of accidental injury

- Water / refreshments and/or snacks for gymnasts

- Buddy system established (no gymnasts go anywhere alone)

VI. **Marketing Materials**

- Club brochures, newsletters, and class schedules

- Special promotion for this show (free class coupon, etc.)

- T-shirts to throw out to section of crowd that cheers loudest

- Contest entry box for free class (to get names & addresses)

VII. **Miscellaneous**

- Rope to mark off exhibition area

- Parents to help with crowd control & gauge audience reaction

- People to help move equipment during the show.

- Parents / Staff to keep kids on track with exhibition

- Notes for changes to make in next exhibition

- Sign re: "next exhibition starts in "? minutes," or at "0:00pm?"

THE ANNOUNCER'S SCRIPT

Unfortunately, I can't actually sit down and write the definitive script for you.

The script will have different elements for different club's strengths and weaknesses or the needs of the particular exhibition.

I can, however, give you the general guidelines to develop your script.

I. The Introduction

Included in this should be a welcoming statement to your audience for coming to the show, a thank you to your hosts for having you there, and the introduction of your team as well as some background information on your program.

II. The Program

Now you must create another sheet titled *"Exhibition Timing / Announcer Script Cues."* Based on what actions are taking place (or the timing) the announcer will be able to read the column marked *"Cue Script Number"* and know what is to be said during that time.

I suggest you take separate sheets of paper or index cards and mark a number or time on each.

The topic on each card will correspond with the activity taking place during the show.

You may also want to designate certain visual cues if the announcer is not familiar with the sport of gymnastics.

The rest is up to you. Decide what you are going to put into your show and what you want the announcer to say during each part.

III. Ending the Show

Thank everyone for attending your exhibition. Thank your hosts. Have your exhibition team come out for one more bow.

Make sure everyone leaves knowing exactly how to get in touch with you to find out more information about your gymnastics facility.

Special Note: Announce the times of any future demonstrations that day or in the near future at which your team will be performing.

IV. Pack Up and Go Home.

Safety Questions to consider in all gymnastics activities

1. Is the gymnastics equipment properly set up, and is the surrounding gymnastics area prepared for the safe performance of gymnastics skills?

2. Is the gymnast physically prepared to do the skill? (I.E. appropriate strength and flexibility)

3. Does the gymnast understand exactly what is expected of him or her in the performance of the skill?

4. Is the gymnast mentally prepared to do the skill?

5. Is the instructor / coach properly prepared to teach / supervise the skill?

This includes an awareness of:

- proper progressions of gymnastics skills and techniques,

- appropriate planning of the event,

- how to safely spot the gymnast,

- how to adapt technique based on gymnast size, shape, and physical ability, as well as performance area constraints.

6. Has the instructor received training and certification in CPR and First Aid?

7. Is there appropriate first aid and safety equipment immediately available including water for proper hydration?

8. Is there an effective communication system in place to notify parents and emergency medical personnel in the event of an athlete injury?

About the Author

Thirty years and thirty thousand pizza's ago, Rik Feeney was a competitive gymnast through High School and college. During his career, Rik owned and worked at private gymnastics clubs where he trained gymnasts from state to national level competitors.

Rik is the author of several books on the sport of gymnastics, self-publishing, and various other topics.

You can find Rik's books on Amazon.com and other online booksellers.

www.ingramcontent.com/pod-product-compliance
Lightning Source LLC
Chambersburg PA
CBHW071737020426
42331CB00008B/2063